THE HINDENBURG
DISASTER

Essential Events

THE HINDENBURG
DISASTER

BY JILL SHERMAN

Content Consultant
Dr. Guillaume de Syon
History Department, Albright College

ABDO
Publishing Company

CREDITS

Published by ABDO Publishing Company, 8000 West 78th Street, Edina, Minnesota 55439. Copyright © 2010 by Abdo Consulting Group, Inc. International copyrights reserved in all countries. No part of this book may be reproduced in any form without written permission from the publisher. The Essential Library™ is a trademark and logo of ABDO Publishing Company.

Printed in the United States of America,
North Mankato, Minnesota
092009
012010

 PRINTED ON RECYCLED PAPER

Editor: Mari Kesselring
Copy Editor: Paula Lewis
Interior Design and Production: Rebecca Daum
Cover Design: Rebecca Daum

Library of Congress Cataloging-in-Publication Data
Sherman, Jill.
  The Hindenburg disaster / Jill Sherman.
      p. cm. — (Essential events)
  Includes bibliographical references and index.
  ISBN 978-1-60453-944-8
  1. Hindenburg (Airship)—Juvenile literature. 2. Aircraft accidents—New Jersey—Juvenile literature. 3. Airships—Germany—Juvenile literature. I. Title.
  TL659.H5S53 2010
  363.12'4—dc22

                              2009030427

TABLE OF CONTENTS

Herbert Morrison, left, broadcasted during the Hindenburg disaster.

OH! THE HUMANITY!

"*W*ell here it comes, ladies and gentlemen, we're out now, outside of the hangar, and what a great sight it is . . . it's a marvelous sight."[1]

On May 6, 1937, radio announcer Herbert Morrison was the only radio reporter on site outside Lakehurst Naval Air Station in New Jersey. He was on assignment for WLS radio in Chicago, Illinois. Morrison was surrounded by photographers, newspaper reporters, and spectators who had gathered to witness the *Hindenburg*'s first landing of the flight season. The zeppelin had made ten trips to the United States the previous year. But its massive form and unique presence in the sky still commanded the public's attention. The hydrogen-filled airship was a marvel of modern engineering, and plans for new airships were already in the works.

Storms in the area had prevented the *Hindenburg* from landing until after 6:00 p.m. The ground crew of 231 men waited to bring in the airship. With an overall length of 804 feet (245 m), the airship would

Airships

Airships, or dirigibles, are essentially powered balloons that contain fins and runners for steering. The engines provide thrust. Rigid German airships were known as zeppelins. They were the most well-designed airships of their day. Rigid airships have a solid internal structure that helps the airship maintain its shape. Today, nonrigid airships, called blimps, are sometimes used. But rigid airships lost their popularity after the *Hindenburg* disaster.

be guided to a docking structure called a mooring mast. The airship had been scheduled to dock earlier, but Captain Max Pruss decided to wait out the storms and took his passengers on a sightseeing tour down the New Jersey shore. An hour later, the storms had died down. Captain Pruss finally had an opportunity to land the airship.

THE EXPLOSION

As Captain Pruss made the final approach to Lakehurst, the ground crew moved into action. The crowd watched expectantly for the *Hindenburg* to make its landing. Photographers began snapping shots of the famous silver airship.

At 6:25 p.m., the airship's crew dropped the landing lines. It quickly became clear that something was wrong. Morrison, who had been narrating the landing for a radio broadcast, described the scene as it unfolded:

Hydrogen

All airships outside the United States, including German zeppelins, used hydrogen gas to make their airships float. Hydrogen gas is lighter than air, but it is highly flammable. A single spark could start an explosion. German engineers believed they had the gas under control. Many safety precautions were taken. It was important that the hydrogen stayed uncontaminated. Any leaks in the hydrogen cells of the airship would be directed up—away from the motors and other mechanical parts of the airship.

It's starting to rain again, the rain had slacked up a little bit, the back motors of the ship are just holding it just enough to keep it from—it burst into flame! It burst into flame and it's falling, it's fire, watch it, watch it, get out of the way, get out of the way, . . . this is one of the worst catastrophes in the world, oh the flames are rising, oh, four or five hundred feet into the sky. It's a terrific crash, ladies and gentlemen, the smoke and its flames now and the frame is crashing to the ground, not quite to the mooring mast, oh the humanity, and all the passengers. Screaming around me, I'm so—I can't even talk, the people, it's not fair, it's—it's—oh! I can't talk, ladies and gentlemen, honest, it's a flaming mass of smoking wreckage, and everybody can hardly breathe.[2]

Smoke filled the air and the *Hindenburg* was engulfed in fire. At one point, Morrison became so horrified that he was unable to continue

Herbert Morrison's Broadcast

Herbert Morrison was the only radio reporter at Lakehurst the night of the *Hindenburg* disaster. Morrison's commentary was not broadcast live, but it was recorded. It was going to be used to promote flights of passenger zeppelins in the midwestern United States.

Morrison's emotional broadcast became famous in the days following the disaster. Some people criticized him for becoming too emotional during the broadcast. Others accused him of exaggerating the extent of the fire because so many of those on board survived. But Morrison claimed that many had praised him for the work he did after the *Hindenburg* exploded. After he recovered from the initial shock, Morrison interviewed survivors and gathered information for the public.

The Hindenburg *exploded and fell to Earth.*

speaking. The crowd watching the landing was
similarly shocked by the explosion. George Willens
and his son were waiting to take the *Hindenburg* on its
return flight to Europe. Willens watched, stunned,
as fire engulfed the airship. Willens said of the
disaster:

> It was all so sudden—so unexpected—so without precedent—
> that for precious moments no one knew what to do or what
> to say. It seemed as if no living thing could pass unscathed
> through that hell of flames—as if all must have perished.[3]

ESCAPE FROM THE AIRSHIP

Despite the enormity of the explosion, many passengers managed to escape the fire. Many described feeling a sudden lurch, which they later learned was the first explosion in the rear of the airship. Initially, the fire did not affect the passenger area, which was near the middle of the airship. However, it was clear to the passengers that something had gone wrong.

After feeling a tremor pass through the airship, passenger Herbert O'Laughlin followed a group out to the promenade. But before he could escape, the airship crashed and O'Laughlin was thrown from the airship. He escaped uninjured and ran from the burning airship.

Joseph Späh, a famous German acrobat, was also on board the airship. After the explosion, he used his camera to smash open a window. Späh and another passenger, Peter Belin, climbed out the window and waited for the airship to come nearer to the ground. Another man joined them, but he was unable to hold on. The man lost his grip, and Späh and Belin watched helplessly as he fell approximately 100 feet (30 m) to his death. Späh and Belin managed to hold on longer and jumped when the airship was approximately 40 feet (12 m) from the ground. Both men survived; the only injury between them was Späh's broken ankle.

Werner Franz, a 14-year-old cabin boy, was in the officers' dining room when the explosion occurred. When the airship crashed to the ground, Franz was unable to find his way out of the fire and wreckage. Franz was saved when a water ballast tank burst above his head. The water drenched the fire surrounding him. Soaking wet, Franz was able to run to safety.

THE WRECKAGE

In just 37 seconds, the mighty *Hindenburg* was reduced to a pile of burning

---

Crew Members Escape

Unlike the passengers, who were confined to a small area in the middle of the airship, crew members were stationed in all areas of the *Hindenburg*.

Four men were stationed in the rear, or stern, of the airship. These men were closest to the area where the fire started and to the first explosion. But as the hydrogen that was keeping the *Hindenburg* afloat escaped, the stern crashed to the ground first. All four members managed to get away.

Twelve crew members were stationed in the nose, or bow, of the airship. As the rear of the airship fell to the ground, the nose rose at a steep angle pointing upward. The men clung to the girders of the ship as the hydrogen cells exploded below them. Only three managed to hold on until the bow reached the ground.

Only five crew members remained at their posts in the control gondola until Pruss ordered everyone to abandon the airship. Captains Pruss and Lehmann left through a window but were met by a wall of flames. Captain Lehmann died the next morning as a result of his injuries.

metal. It would continue to smolder for hours after the crash.

Miraculously, many passengers and crew members escaped the burning airship uninjured. Others escaped with severe burns and injuries. These people were rushed to area hospitals, but many would not recover. A number of others did not escape the fire.

As a result of the *Hindenburg* disaster, 36 people died. Of the 97 people on board, 22 crew members and 13 passengers died, either in the fire, or later as a result of their injuries. One person on the ground died.

In the days following the disaster, many people wondered what had gone wrong. How could the German airship believed to be safe crash so disastrously? What caused the sudden fire? Was it sabotage? An engineering flaw? A result of the storms in the area?

Hindenburg **Facts**

- Length: 804 feet (245 m)
- Width: 135 feet (41 m)
- Weight: 430,956 pounds (195,478 kg)
- Hydrogen capacity: 7 million cubic feet (198,217 m³)
- Maximum capacity: 15,740 pounds (7,139.5439 kg)
- Maximum speed: 85 miles per hour (136.7 km/h)

Though the answers to these questions would remain a mystery for a long time, one thing was clear. The age of the airship had ended abruptly in the tragedy. ⌒

The wreckage of the Hindenburg smoldered for hours after the crash.

Count Zeppelin

Lighter Than Air

German-made airships, or zeppelins, such as the *Hindenburg*, were known for their superior design and flying capabilities. This success was due largely to the work of Count Ferdinand Adolf August Heinrich von Zeppelin.

Count Zeppelin became fascinated with air travel during a visit to St. Paul, Minnesota, where he first rode in an air balloon on August 19, 1863. The memory of that ride stayed with him when he returned to his post as an officer in the German military. But it was not until 1874 that Count Zeppelin first put down his ideas for building a rigid airship.

EARLY AIRSHIPS

By 1874, several unsuccessful attempts at building a maneuverable airship had been made. Hot-air balloons came into use in France around 1783. Shortly thereafter, inventors began imagining ways to control the direction the balloons moved. Plans for balloons pulled by birds, with attached sails, and with winglike "air oars" were unsuccessful.

A French inventor, Henri Giffard, was the first to have any success powering an airship. Giffard invented a steam engine that weighed only 250 pounds (113 kg). The

The Montgolfier Brothers

A lighter-than-air craft was first achieved in the late 1700s. Joseph-Michel and Jacques-Étienne Montgolfier are credited with creating the first hot-air balloon. Because hot air rises, as the air at the bottom opening is heated, it lifts the balloon and attached gondola upward. The Montgolfier brothers lifted their aircraft to a height of 6,000 feet (1,829 m) when they first demonstrated their balloon on June 5, 1783. Those who followed in the brothers' footsteps preferred to try to use hydrogen instead of hot air. Hydrogen helped the balloon stay up longer.

engine was light enough that a balloon could lift it, the fuel, and a passenger. On September 24, 1852, Giffard used his engine to fly an elongated balloon 15.5 miles (25 km). The balloon measured 144 feet (44 m) from end to end. However, the small engine was not powerful enough to overcome strong winds.

In the years following Giffard's flight, airship designers continued to make improvements. They achieved greater degrees of maneuverability and stability. By 1900, Count Zeppelin would bring such improvements to the design of lighter-than-air crafts that airships would be in production by the start of World War I.

THE FOOLISH COUNT

The French made many of the early achievements in the design of airships. Count Zeppelin was eager for Germany to begin its own airship development. He urged King Wilhelm of Württemberg to begin a program. When Zeppelin retired from the military in 1890, he was

La France

Designed by Captain Charles Renard and Captain Arthur Krebs of the French army's balloon corps, *La France* made its first flight in 1884. The nonrigid airship was powered by an electric motor. *La France* was the first airship to have a controlled flight against the wind. Despite this success, batteries to power the motor were a burden on the ship, weighing one-half ton (.45 tonnes) each. The airship's maximum speed was 14 miles per hour (22.5 km/h).

finally able to focus on his ideas for building airships.

Unlike most other airships of the time, Zeppelin's plans called for a rigid design. Unlike nonrigid balloons, rigid airships would not be affected as much by atmospheric pressure. This also allowed airships to be made larger and carry more lifting gas. Zeppelin once said of his design, "My system is the best, the only conceivable one for military purposes and, if airships are possible at all, then mine are possible."[1]

A scientific commission rejected Zeppelin's first two designs. The commission doubted the designs would work. Zeppelin faced ridicule for his efforts. Members of the upper class called him a lunatic and the "foolish count." But in 1896, the Union of German Engineers endorsed one of Zeppelin's designs. Shortly afterward, Zeppelin became aware of the possibilities of using

An Unconventional Leader

Born into aristocracy on July 8, 1838, Count Zeppelin had a long career as a German military officer. He served notably in the Franco-Prussian War and gained a reputation for bravery under fire.

He was also a somewhat unconventional leader. It was considered improper for an officer in the Prussian army to climb a tree to view the lay of the land or to see where other forces were gathered. Zeppelin often insisted on seeing the land for himself. Behavior such as this gained him the respect of those he commanded.

As a devoted military man, Zeppelin saw the use of airships primarily as a military tool. He expected them to be very useful in surveillance, transportation, and bombing.

manufactured aluminum in building his aircraft. Use of this lightweight material in constructing the girders would make it easier to lift the ship. Zeppelin partnered with aluminum maker Carl Berg and began construction of his first lighter-than-air craft.

The LZ 1

Work on the *Luftschiff*, or airship, began in 1898. Two years later, the Luftschiff Zeppelin One (LZ 1) was complete. The LZ 1 was built in a floating shed on Lake Constance near Menzell, Germany. It contained two passenger cars and used two 14.7 horsepower engines.

The 416-foot (127-m) ship took its maiden flight on July 2, 1900. The ship flew for 18 minutes. Military observers were unimpressed by the airship's brief flight.

The LZ 1 flew two more times before Zeppelin ran out of money. He dismantled the airship and sold the pieces for scrap. Zeppelin kept three employees on afterward—two

The Deutsch Prize

The Deutsch Prize was awarded to Alberto Santos-Dumont in 1901. He successfully flew an airship from St. Cloud, France, to the Eiffel Tower and back in less than 30 minutes. The flight won him world fame, as well as the cash prize of 100,000 francs ($20,000 at that time).

Zeppelin LZ 3

night watchmen and an engineer. Without the
backing of the German military to improve the
design, Zeppelin was left to raise funds on his own
to build a new airship.

A National Endeavor

Zeppelin's next three airships, the LZ 2,
the LZ 3, and the LZ 4, were measurably more
successful. The LZ 2 was wrecked in a windstorm.
The LZ 3 made its first flight in October 1906.

When the LZ 3 successfully made an eight-hour trip in 1907, the public began to take notice of the eccentric count.

The LZ 4 was first tested in 1908 with a 12-hour flight over Switzerland. Next, the LZ 4 was to make a 24-hour nonstop flight. The ship was forced to land for repairs twice. After the second stop for repairs in Echterdingen, Germany, disaster struck. The airship was tied up at the airfield when a strong wind picked the LZ 4 up from its moorings. The crew guarding the airship tried to bring it back to

Meeting with Hugo Eckener

Working for the *Frankfurter Zeitung*, a German newspaper, Hugo Eckener covered test flights of both the LZ 1 and the LZ 2. Eckener's reports were somewhat critical of the aircrafts, whose test flights were unimpressive. The LZ 2 crashed during the flight Eckener observed in October 1906.

Count Zeppelin called on Eckener at home a few weeks after the crash of the LZ 2. The count corrected a few inaccurate points Eckener had made in his article about the LZ 2. He also invited him to dinner. Zeppelin had faced harsher criticism of his airships from other newspapers and sensed that Eckener was sympathetic to his work. Eckener found Zeppelin to be rather likeable. By the end of the meal, Eckener offered to help publicize Zeppelin's projects.

As Eckener continued to follow the progress of the Zeppelin Company, he became more interested in airships. Eckener was hired as a full-time director of public relations in 1908. In 1909, Zeppelin and Eckener became business partners when they cofounded Deutsche Luftschiffahrts-Aktien-Gesellschaft, the first passenger airline.

the ground, but the LZ 4 crashed into a tree. The hydrogen-filled ship exploded. Count Zeppelin was deeply disappointed by the destruction of this airship. He would not be able to afford to build another.

But in a turn of fortune, the German people came to Count Zeppelin's rescue. Donations and letters asking the count to continue to build his airships began pouring in. Many came from wealthy donors. But Zeppelin also received donations from the Mining Association of Essen, a bowling club, and a young girl. All of Germany, it seemed, was behind Zeppelin and his airships.

THE ZEPPELIN COMPANY

Zeppelin received 6 million deutsche marks from donations (approximately $1.5 million in U.S. currency). He used the money to start the Zeppelin Company in September 1908. He hired Carl Berg's son-in-law Alfred Colsman as the business manager, and Hugo Eckener came on as the director of public relations.

Fueled by orders from Germany's army, the Zeppelin Company produced the LZ 5 and reproduced the LZ 3. Zeppelin and Eckener then founded the *Deutsche Luftschiffahrts-Aktien-Gesellschaft* (DELAG), or the "German Airship Transport Company," in 1909. Though Zeppelin believed his airships were more valuable for military use, transportation service would prove to be a valuable source of income for the company.

Despite having very little flight experience, Eckener was promoted to DELAG flight director. An early accident with the LZ 8 made Eckener a cautious pilot, and he would stress the need for caution to the pilots he trained. Many people were impressed with the success of the Zeppelin Company. From 1911 to 1914, DELAG would make 1,588 passenger flights without a single passenger injury. The easily maneuverable aircrafts and well-trained pilots helped put Germany in a good position for what was to come next.

Hugo Eckener circa 1924

French soldiers inspected a crashed zeppelin in 1913.

WAR MACHINE

Under the cover of nightfall, three German navy airships began their quiet flight up the English coast. The ships left their base at Nordholz on the morning of January 19, 1915, on a mission ordered by Kaiser Wilhelm II. The L 3, the L 4, and the L 6 were to bomb British shipyards on England's northern coast.

The crew of the L 6 was forced to abandon its mission because of a mechanical failure, but the L 3 and the L 4 continued on. German zeppelins could fly at a height of 20,000 feet (6,096 m)—well out of the range of ground ammunition. British airplanes were not equipped to fend off the zeppelins. Even if pilots were lucky enough to puncture a zeppelin's outer cover and release the hydrogen, the airship's other hydrogen cells contained more than enough gas to keep it afloat.

When the L 3 and the L 4 came in over the coast of Great Yarmouth, England, their captains gave the orders to release the bombs. The ground flashed in light. The unsuspecting people awoke terrified by the explosions surrounding them.

The ships had missed their target by miles. The L 3 bombed a smaller port than intended. The L 4 hit several villages nearby. Four civilians died in the attacks. And though the

World War I

World War I broke out in Europe in 1914 after the assassination of Archduke Franz Ferdinand, heir to the Austro-Hungarian Empire. Military alliances brought much of Europe together in the conflict. The Entente Powers, commonly referred to as the Allies, were made up of Serbia, France, Russia, and the United Kingdom. The Austro-Hungarian Empire and Germany were the Central Powers. Other countries later joined each side. The United States joined the allies in 1917. U.S. troops and resources helped bring the war to an end in 1918.

bombings inflicted some damage, the mission had missed all of its military targets.

This attack, however, surprised British citizens who had not considered zeppelins dangerous. This bombing also set the stage for the role German zeppelins would play in World War I.

The Outbreak of the War

Count Zeppelin had always believed that the true usefulness of his airships lay in the military. So when World War I broke out in 1914, Zeppelin began to prepare his airships for war.

Germany's army and navy began the war with 11 airships. However, these were not much different from passenger airships. They were not suited for the demands of war. In one year, Germany's army had lost all but four of its airships in accidents and crashes.

Zeppelin Song

The German people were proud of their superior airships. They hoped the zeppelins would win the war for Germany. School children even sang a song about the mighty zeppelins:

"Fly, Zeppelin,
Help us in the war,
Fly to England,
England will be destroyed by fire,
Fly Zeppelin."[1]

In 1918, a zeppelin raid destroyed part of a hospital in London.

The Zeppelin Company would produce a total of 88 airships for the German military during the war, far more than any of its competitors. Zeppelin's airships could fly higher than other airships of the day. They were also outfitted with machine guns to fend off attacking airplanes. The airships proved to be useful in scouting missions and transportation as well. According to Count Zeppelin, "War in the air is here—and here to stay."[2]

Effect of Zeppelin Air Raids

The success of Germany's zeppelins in air raids is questionable. The zeppelins were largely ineffective for military offense. The attacks did not result in great strategic damage to Germany's enemies. But the army continued to order more attacks. They believed that the attacks made people fearful. German leaders hoped that countries would use their resources to defend their cities against the zeppelins, rather than other parts of the war effort.

However, the air raids may have had an opposite effect. The raids mostly killed civilians, so they were useful in promoting the war effort in England. Men angered by the attacks enlisted in large numbers.

Other countries also had airships. Britain had approximately 200 nonrigid airships, or blimps, during the war. But unlike Germany, other countries used their airships mainly for defensive purposes. Although Germany's airships did not inflict much physical damage, they became effective on a psychological level.

"Baby Killers"

The first zeppelin air raids were unsuccessful, but they attracted attention. England used the air raids to help recruit men to join the army. They publicized the zeppelins as "baby killers" because the attacks hurt innocent civilians. The attacks were unnerving because they were so difficult to defend against.

Although Germany's air raids became more successful, some causing considerable damage to its enemies, it remained difficult for bombers to hit their targets. The zeppelins flew at a great height to avoid detection and to stay out of range of a defensive attack. Zeppelin bombers mainly caused damage to civilian property. Over the course of the war, approximately 2,000 people in Britain were injured or killed during air raids.

DEFEAT OF THE MILITARY AIRSHIP

After months of aerial attacks, the British managed to destroy a zeppelin bomber on June 7, 1915. Flight Sub-Lieutenant Reginald Warneford flew his small plane over the LZ 37 and dropped six bombs on the airship. The bombs blasted a hole in the ship's cover, and the hydrogen-filled zeppelin exploded.

Though this success was cause for celebration in Britain, it was difficult to continue attacks such as this. The zeppelins usually took English cities by surprise, allowing little time for the British to launch a defensive

London Air Raid

On the night of September 8, 1915, Lieutenant Heinrich Mathy led an aerial bombing attack on London. Mathy commanded the L 13 as it took London by surprise. The crew of the L 13 dropped several large bombs on warehouses and Liverpool Street Station. Mathy's attack was the most devastating aerial attack during the war. It killed 22 people.

attack before the zeppelin raid had ended. Fighter pilots also had trouble catching the high-flying zeppelins.

But the British would not remain at the mercy of the zeppelins. Brighter searchlights helped the British spot approaching zeppelins. They also developed airplanes that could fly more easily at higher altitudes on a level with the zeppelins. These planes were also armed with incendiary bullets. The bullets were coated with phosphorus that burns in air. When these bullets broke through the outer cover of the zeppelins, they ignited the hydrogen within. These explosions

Zeppelins and the Treaty of Versailles

At the war's end, Germany signed a peace treaty with the allied nations. These nations included England, France, Italy, and Japan. The Treaty of Versailles, signed on June 28, 1919, required Germany to pay war reparations. In part, these reparations required Germany to give up its surviving zeppelins. Germany was also required to limit the size of its military and was prohibited from building new airships.

At the end of the war, Germany had 14 airships. But upon hearing that Germany would have to surrender its zeppelins, a group of German citizens broke into the airship sheds and destroyed six of the remaining airships. The eight remaining airships were distributed among the allied nations.

The United States, which did not ratify the Treaty of Versailles, signed a separate treaty with Germany. This treaty required Germany to build an airship for the United States that would be able to cross the Atlantic Ocean. Because this airship was not for the German military, the allied nations permitted the Zeppelin Company to build it.

were especially deadly to the German crew inside. In order to save weight, wartime zeppelins did not carry parachutes.

Though Germany continued to launch air raids, the crews operating the zeppelins were well aware that the large aircrafts had become incredibly vulnerable to attacks. Some were not lucky enough to escape the attacks. According to zeppelin Lieutenant Henrich Mathy,

> It is only a question of time before we join the rest. . . . If anyone should say that he was not haunted by visions of burning airships, then he would be a braggart.[3]

Count Zeppelin was also disappointed that so many of his airships were lost in battle. Although Zeppelin died on March 8, 1917, before the worst of the attacks against the zeppelins occurred, he worried that airships would never be the military weapons he had hoped.

Germany lost the war, and some of its remaining zeppelins were destroyed on the ground. It was forced to surrender the other zeppelins. These were distributed among the winning allied nations, who hoped to use the zeppelin designs to develop airship programs of their own. The Zeppelin Company was no longer allowed to produce airships. However, in 1922 the rules would change. The Zeppelin Company would build a transoceanic airship for the United States. ⌒

Magazines and posters depicted the attitude that the British had toward zeppelins during World War I.

The British airship R 34 made the first nonstop ocean crossing.

THE FUTURE
OF AIR TRAVEL

The prestige of achieving the first transatlantic airship flight would not go to Germany, but to England. In July 1919, England's R 34, a near copy of Germany's captured L 33, made the first nonstop ocean crossing.

Airship Failures

Despite this success, England's airship program failed to progress much further. All of England's remaining airships were destroyed in accidents during the 1920s, and the government mostly abandoned the expensive airship program. England did continue, however, to develop passenger airships.

France and Italy faced similar difficulties developing military airships. France's *Dixmude* disappeared over the Mediterranean Sea in 1923 with 50 people on board. Italy built the *Roma* and sold it to the United States. The *Roma* crashed in Virginia in 1922, killing 33 of the 44 people on board. Italian airships also explored the North Pole. But after one of their airships crashed and the crew had to be rescued, Italy stopped building airships.

The United States built its own airship, the *Shenandoah*, during this

The Fate of the *Dixmude*

The French government received Germany's L 72 after the war and renamed it the *Dixmude*. The ship was sent on a flight on December 18, 1923, but disappeared over the Mediterranean Sea. The commander's body and a few bits of wreckage were eventually recovered.

Since its disappearance, people have speculated on what exactly happened to the *Dixmude*. Because more wreckage was never found, some people sensationally claimed that the control gondola broke off but that the rest of the airship continued on. They suggested that the passengers and crew could be living somewhere in Africa. However, most people believe that the airship was destroyed in a storm.

period as well. This was the first airship designed to use helium as the lifting gas. After the *Roma* disaster, the United States would not fly a hydrogen-filled airship again. The *Shenandoah* made its first flight on September 4, 1923, from the new air station in Lakehurst, New Jersey. The *Shenandoah* made several successful flights, and the U.S. Navy hailed it as the strongest airship in the world. But during a flight over the Midwest on September 3, 1925, the *Shenandoah*'s crew struggled to control the airship when it experienced strong winds. The ship's hull snapped in two, and the airship crashed in Ohio. Of the 43 men on board, 14 died.

THE LZ 126

Meanwhile, the Zeppelin Company finished building the LZ 126 for the U.S. Navy. Although the airship was being

Expedition to the North Pole

Italy's airship program was notable for its exploration of the Arctic. In 1926, despite battling severe weather, the 348-foot (106-m) semirigid *Norge* returned safely from the North Pole. The *Italia*, sent in 1928, was not as lucky. On May 25, the airship made a crash landing in the Arctic. The crew radioed for help, but it took weeks to be rescued. On July 12, a Russian icebreaker finally reached the men—49 days after the crash. Of the 16 men on board the *Italia*, 8 survived the ordeal.

Hugo Eckener, center, and his crew flew the Los Angeles.

built for the U.S. Navy to use as a training ship, international laws following World War I required that the airship be built for commercial rather than military purposes. The airship had passenger accommodations. The size of the airship was also restricted. The postwar laws allowed a maximum gas capacity of 1 million cubic feet (28,317 m³). However, the United States was able to stretch the rules and the LZ 126 was permitted a gas capacity of 2.5 million cubic feet (70,792 m³).

Eckener delivered the LZ 126 to Lakehurst Naval Air Station on October 15, 1924. It was soon renamed the *Los Angeles.* Though the *Los Angeles* was able to make transatlantic crossings, the United States would not use it for such trips. The *Los Angeles* was a smaller airship than the United States originally wanted. Also, the United States had large stores of helium, which it wanted to use as the lifting gas. Because of its size, the *Los Angeles* was not a good airship for long flights. Helium has less lifting power than hydrogen, and it was not possible to refuel in Europe on transatlantic crossings.

The *Los Angeles* served the U.S. Navy well. The ship was used for military flights and scientific research. It was the only airship to be moored on

Helium

Hydrogen is the only element lighter than helium. Helium is an inert gas. Unlike hydrogen, it does not combine with air to become flammable. The United States discovered large deposits of natural gas in its soil from which helium could be extracted at a relatively small cost. For the United States, this made helium the ideal gas to use in its airships. Although more expensive than hydrogen, helium seemed a better choice for safety reasons.

an aircraft carrier. Its years of accident-free service helped convince many people of the superiority of the Zeppelin Company's airships.

The Graf Zeppelin

Germany's restrictions on building airships were finally lifted in spring of 1926. Eckener began raising money and making plans to build a new luxury airship. The LZ 127 would have all the luxuries of an ocean liner and restore Germany's place as the leader in airship design. Eckener said of the

The R 101 Disaster

In 1929, the same year that the *Graf Zeppelin* flew around the world, two companies in England were building passenger airships. The makers of the R 100 and the R 101 were in stiff competition with each other. The makers of the R 101 knew the airship had some flaws. But when the R 101 was scheduled to make a well-publicized flight to India in 1930, they went ahead with the flight to prove the superiority of the R 101 over the R 100.

The R 101 took off for India on October 4, 1930. Almost immediately, the airship ran into poor weather. Rain and winds up to 50 miles per hour (80.5 km/h) made the flight difficult to control, and the ship lost one of its engines. Rather than turn around, the airship's captains made the decision to continue on in order to arrive on schedule.

In the early morning of October 5, as the airship was flying over the French countryside, the R 101 began to dive. The crew corrected the airship, but once again it dove toward the ground and crashed. Of the 56 people on board, only 6 survived.

The British people were shocked by the disaster, and thousands mourned the dead. The British government soon canceled all plans for future airships, and the R 100 was dismantled. England would never fly another rigid airship.

ship, "She was to be an airship in which one would not merely fly, but would also be able to voyage."[1]

The LZ 127 was named in honor of Count, or *Graf*, Zeppelin. On September 18, 1928, the *Graf Zeppelin* was unveiled. It made its first ocean crossing to the United States in October 1928. The ship arrived in New York to a cheering crowd. Captain Ernst Lehmann said of the arrival of the *Graf Zeppelin* to the United States:

> *The masses of people went mad with enthusiasm; factory sirens were blowing, locomotive and steam whistles shrilled out; the automobiles blew their horns, and a veritable storm of confetti and paper streamers fell from the windows of the skyscrapers.*[2]

Graf Zeppelin Facts

- Length: 775 feet (236 m)
- Height: 110 feet (34 m)
- Hydrogen capacity: 3,037,000 cubic feet (85,998 m³)
- Maximum speed: 105 miles per hour (169 km/h)
- Passenger limit: 20

In the United States, Eckener was looking to find a partner with whom to build a commercial transatlantic airline with four larger airships. Although the *Graf Zeppelin* had attracted great enthusiasm for airships, he could not find a backer.

Eckener decided to arrange a passenger flight around the world. The profits from this flight would be used to finance his airline.

Around the World

The cost of a ticket for the famous flight would be equal to $55,000 in today's currency. Eckener also sold exclusive press rights to cover the well-publicized flight. William Randolph Hearst paid $100,000 for the English-language rights, an amazing sum at the time. Stamp collectors paid to have their mail carried on board the *Graf Zeppelin* during the historic flight. The mail was stamped as having been carried on the flight and postmarked at Lakehurst, New Jersey; Friedrichshafen, Germany; Tokyo, Japan; and Los Angeles, California.

The flight left Lakehurst on August 7, 1929, and took 22 days to complete. The *Graf Zeppelin* was warmly received wherever it traveled. People followed the airship's progress with excitement and enthusiasm. One eyewitness estimated that nearly 4 million people flooded the streets of Tokyo to witness the *Graf Zeppelin*'s long-awaited arrival. A ceremony was held to celebrate the airship's arrival. Several journalists were on board to report the events of the flight.

The *Graf Zeppelin* returned to Lakehurst on August 29, completing the first round-the-world flight. The next day, New York City held a ticker-tape parade in celebration of the *Graf Zeppelin*'s successful flight. President Herbert Hoover attended a ceremony in Eckener's honor. Hoover remarked, "I thought the day of the great adventures, like Columbus, Vasco da Gama, and Magellan, was in the past. Now I know such an adventurer is in my presence."[3]

Graf Zeppelin *flew over Tokyo, Japan, during its trip around the world.*

The Hindenburg *was built in Germany.*

THE GREATEST AIRSHIP

olstered by the success of the *Graf Zeppelin*, Eckener was determined to build an even larger airship and begin his airline. But when the New York stock market crashed on October 24, 1929, only two months after the *Graf*

Zeppelin's historic flight around the globe, the world's economy began to suffer.

It was not until 1933 that Eckener received financial support for his airship. Adolf Hitler and the Nazi Party had come to power in Germany. The Nazi Party wanted to show the world Germany's superior engineering with a bigger and better zeppelin.

BUILDING THE LZ 129

Though Eckener did not support the Nazi Party, he knew they were the only likely source of financial backing. Eckener began work on the LZ 129 in 1932. A new air hangar was built to contain the huge airship. With a few improvements, the LZ 129 was similar to the *Graf Zeppelin* in design.

The LZ 129 was 804 feet (245 m) long and larger than any other airship. Its engines were powered by diesel fuel. This gas reduced the risk of fire. Huge

Helium or Hydrogen

The LZ 129 was designed to be able to use helium. Eckener thought that it would be safer that way. Also, because Germany would have to buy helium from the United States, he believed it would improve relations between the two countries.

Ernst Lehmann, an airship captain for the Zeppelin Company, preferred using hydrogen. He thought that the Zeppelin Company had proven its ability to control the flammable gas. Germany had not had a serious accident because of hydrogen gas. Also, buying helium from the United States would be much more costly than using hydrogen.

Eckener agreed that the gas was well controlled. Though helium would be safer, he did not consider the use of hydrogen gas to be a serious problem.

round rings made of a lightweight aluminum, called duralumin, divided the ship into 16 separate compartments for the hydrogen lifting gas. Each gastight bag was separated from the one next to it by a cotton lining. The outer cover of the LZ 129 was coated with a new reflective doping compound to strengthen the fabric cover. The doping also gave the ship a silvery color.

The LZ 129 had another notable difference from other zeppelins. All of the areas that carried the passengers and the crew were inside the airship's body. Other airships had hanging gondolas in which the passengers and airship captains stayed. With these design changes, the *Hindenburg* was born.

The Nazi Party

The Nazi Party saw zeppelins as tools to deliver propaganda messages to German citizens. The *Hindenburg* was no exception. It took its first trial flight on March 4, 1936. Then, on March 26, 1936, Dr. Goebbels, the propaganda minister for the Nazi Party, required the use of the *Graf Zeppelin* and the *Hindenburg* to fly over German cities and drop leaflets in support of Hitler. As the *Hindenburg* was being removed from its hangar, a gust of wind lifted the airship up, out of the control of the ground crew, and slammed it into the ground. The *Hindenburg*'s tail fin and lower rudder were damaged, and the outer canvas was torn.

When Eckener heard what had happened to the ship, he was outraged. Eckener berated Captain Ernst Lehmann for his lack of caution. Eckener believed the propaganda tour was a waste of time and certainly not something worth risking the airship.

Word of the argument between Lehmann and Eckener got back to Goebbels. The propaganda

Nazi Germany

In the late 1920s, Germany faced increased economic pressures, as did much of the world. Adolf Hitler and the Nazi Party called for government reform. The Nazis encouraged nationalism and promised to restore Germany to greatness. Hitler became chancellor of Germany in 1933. He quickly assumed full control of the government, and he controlled the media and schools as well.

The Nazis used their control over the media to spread propaganda in favor of their party. This propaganda praised the Nazi Party's work, encouraged military training, and promoted national pride. The Nazis also ranked German Jews and anyone who would not conform to Nazi beliefs as second-class citizens. The Nazis realized that the *Graf Zeppelin* and the *Hindenburg* would be excellent propaganda tools. They used them to spread literature about the party.

This propaganda helped Hitler rebuild Germany's army. In 1938, the Nazis invaded Austria and Czechoslovakia. It became clear that Hitler intended to take over more territory, and Europe was again in the midst of war. World War II began on September 1, 1939, when Germany invaded Poland.

minister declared Eckener a "nonperson." The radio, newspapers, and other media were banned from mentioning the popular director of the Zeppelin Company or printing his image. However, Eckener was so popular in Germany that the ban was eventually repealed.

The Nazi Party continued to use the *Graf Zeppelin* and the *Hindenburg* for propaganda missions. In accordance with German law at the time, the tail fins of both airships were painted to display the swastika, a symbol of the Nazi Party. Though he strongly disagreed with the Nazis, Eckener was helpless to prevent them from using his airships.

First Flight Season

On March 31, 1936, the *Hindenburg* made its first flight to Rio de Janeiro, Brazil. Eckener was on board as a passenger, and Ernst Lehmann captained the ship. During the flight out and the return flight, several of the *Hindenburg*'s engines failed and needed to be repaired. Eckener believed that this potentially dangerous failure might have been avoided. When the

The Olympics

Berlin hosted the 1936 Summer Olympics. As part of the opening ceremonies, Hitler wanted to show off the *Hindenburg*. The airship passed over the stadium, taking the crowd's attention away from the events on the field.

The Nazi Party used the Hindenburg *for propaganda tours.*

Hindenburg had been used on propaganda flights,
Eckener felt it should have been undergoing stress
tests. After the *Hindenburg* made it home safely, all
four of its engines were overhauled. The *Hindenburg*'s
first flight to the United States left Germany on
May 6, 1936. Thousands of spectators were on site to
watch the airship make its first passenger flight. Many
journalists were on board this historic trip. Those
who had been on the *Graf Zeppelin* were impressed

with the large passenger areas and the luxurious accommodations. Tests had shown that inside the ship, a wine bottle would tip over if the airship tilted at a ten-degree angle. The captains were instructed not to allow the ship to tilt at more than five degrees. This made the *Hindenburg* a remarkably smooth ride. For two hours, one passenger did not realize that the ship had taken off. Louis Lochner, a reporter on the flight, remarked, "You feel as though you are carried in the arms of angels."[1]

Airmail

The *Hindenburg* also proved useful in delivering airmail. The airship's crew was able to drop large bags of mail at various cities that it flew over. Airship mail delivery was especially popular in Brazil. The *Hindenburg* even had its own post office. A letter postmarked by the *Hindenburg* is greatly desired among stamp collectors.

After a mere two-and-a-half days of flying, the *Hindenburg* passed over New York City and was greeted with cheers from the crowd below. The airship docked safely at Lakehurst. Though Eckener was a "nonperson" in his home country, he was bombarded by reporters in the United States. Eckener thanked President Roosevelt for his help in making transatlantic airship service possible. The *Hindenburg* would complete ten round-trip flights from Europe to the United States that flight season.

The *Hindenburg* also made seven flights to Rio de Janeiro in 1936. During the winter months, the weather did not permit easy air travel to North America. In the early winter, the airship made flights to Brazil, which had a large German population. In some parts of South America, the weather was so mild that it made the air hangars unnecessary. But during the coldest parts of winter, the *Hindenburg* remained in an air hangar for upgrades and maintenance.

Speed

The *Hindenburg* flew at a maximum speed of 85 miles per hour (137 km/h), and it could complete a flight from Europe to the United States in a little more than two days. By comparison, a transatlantic crossing by ocean liner, the only other option at the time, took nearly a week.

This first flight season was a remarkable success. The *Hindenburg* gained a reputation for its reliability and its comfortable flights. In its first year of operation, the ship carried 1,600 transatlantic passengers and traveled a total of 200,000 miles (321,869 km). Passenger-ticket sales were up, and postal service by airship was incredibly desirable.

The *Hindenburg* had proven that transatlantic airship service was popular. The Zeppelin Company began working on a plan to expand airship service to more parts of the world. They hoped to have as many as 40 giant airships operating by 1945. The *Hindenburg* was also remodeled to include ten additional passenger cabins. The second flight season offered 18 round-trip flights from Europe to North America. The first of these flights was scheduled to leave on May 3, 1937.

The Hindenburg was kept at Lakehurst after its first flight to the United States in 1936.

German ambassador Hans Luther felt it was necessary to search the Hindenburg *for bombs.*

Up Ship!

s the *Hindenburg* crew members prepared for their first flight of the 1937 season to the United States, they were informed that the security of the airship might be in question. The *Hindenburg* was often viewed as a symbol of the Nazi

Party. As such, it attracted a good deal of negative attention. The airship needed to be guarded at all times to prevent sabotage.

Shortly before the *Hindenburg* was to make its first flight to the United States for the season, the German embassy to the United States had received a letter warning of a bomb on board the *Hindenburg*. Kathie Rauch of Milwaukee, Wisconsin, wrote the letter. Rauch wrote,

> *Please inform the Zeppelin company in Frankfurt-am-Main that they should open and search all mail before it is put on board prior to every flight of the Zeppelin Hindenburg. The Zeppelin is going to be destroyed by a time bomb during its flight to another country.* [1]

The Search

Although the embassy received letters such as Rauch's from time to time, Hans Luther, Germany's ambassador, thought this one was worth looking into. The day before the *Hindenburg* was to depart, German security troops arrived at Frankfurt to search the airship.

Cost of a Flight

A ticket to cross the Atlantic on the *Hindenburg* cost $400 in 1936. That was equal to the price of a small car bought that year.

The Nazis suspected that if a bomb were placed inside the *Hindenburg*, it would likely have been put there by a crew member. They used their own men to search the airship. However, the security troops were unfamiliar with the enormous airship. If a bomb were inside the *Hindenburg*, it was unlikely that the security troops would find anything. Because the hydrogen gas cells were already inflated at the time of the search, it would have been impossible for the troops to reach several parts of the airship.

As the *Hindenburg* was being searched, Captain Lehmann received a copy of Rauch's letter. Lehmann had more experience working on airships than the other crew members. If something were to go wrong, Lehmann wanted to be there. He volunteered to go along on the trip.

THE PASSENGERS ARRIVE

The search turned up nothing suspicious. As part of its regular process, the Zeppelin Company inspected the passengers' belongings as they boarded the ship. Nothing that caused a spark was allowed. A spark risked the possibility of igniting the hydrogen that kept the airship in the air. Matches, lighters, and batteries were banned.

However, the inspection this day was more thorough than usual. Each piece of luggage was X-rayed, opened, and inspected. Gifts were unwrapped and inspected. Perfumes were opened and smelled for potentially dangerous chemicals. Camera equipment was confiscated.

Eventually, all the passengers were allowed on board the airship. And at 8:15 p.m., the *Hindenburg* began its flight. A band played the German national anthem, and the passengers

Suspicious Passengers

The Nazis were fearful of a sabotage on board the *Hindenburg*. They looked closely at a number of passengers on the May 3 flight. Major Hufschmidt had a file prepared on everyone who would be on the flight. He advised members of the Nazi security who would be flying on the *Hindenburg* and pointed out which passengers to watch.

Leonard and Gertrude Adelt were journalists, and they were flying free of charge on the *Hindenburg*. Gertrude was under suspicion because she had written unflattering articles about the Nazi Party. The Adelts were also friends with Stefan Zweig, a vocal opponent of the Nazis.

Joseph Späh, an acrobat, had several friends who were known opponents of the Nazi Party. As an acrobat, Späh might be able to climb into parts of the airship that were off limits to passengers and plant a bomb.

Carl Clemens, a photographer, was flying at a reduced fare. Heinz Wronsky, a former Nazi member, had arranged his fare. There was concern that Wronsky might be angry with the Nazi Party and collaborate with Clemens to sabotage the airship. Clemens's camera equipment and flash bulbs were confiscated before he boarded the flight.

Edward Douglas, an advertising agent with General Motors, was suspected of being a spy. He too was considered dangerous.

Passengers were not permitted to leave the passenger area unaccompanied. The first night of the flight, however, Joseph Späh persuaded a crew member to take him to his dog so he could feed her.

The next day, Späh took a guided tour of portions of the airship's interior with several other passengers. When the tour passed the animal hold, Späh deviated from the tour to spend some time with his pet. He later rejoined the tour and was warned against leaving again. However, Späh went into the ship's interior a third time to get some exercise.

After that, security considered confining him to his cabin for the remainder of the flight.

waved to the crowd below as the *Hindenburg* left Germany for the last time.

On Board the *Hindenburg*

Once they were allowed on board the *Hindenburg*, the passengers experienced the luxury of the massive airship. Both sides of the passenger level had large, open promenades with windows that could be opened. Passengers spent much of their time on the promenade watching the scenery pass below them. Typically, the *Hindenburg* flew at a relatively low altitude, and passengers could see the people on the ground. The walls were painted with murals. One wall contained a world map so passengers could chart the *Hindenburg*'s progress.

Passengers could retreat to a quiet writing room and use special *Hindenburg* stationery to write letters. A smoking room was available on the lower deck. The room was pressurized and air locked to keep hydrogen out.

Food was prepared in a kitchen on board the Hindenburg.

An attendant stood watch at the door and allowed passengers into the room. He was also the only one on board the ship allowed to carry a lighter or matches. It was his responsibility to ensure that passengers did not leave the room with any lit embers.

The passengers' private rooms were an improvement over the *Graf Zeppelin*. Each room contained two bunk beds, a sink, and a writing table that could be folded up against the wall. Passengers could leave their shoes in the hallway outside their rooms to be polished and returned by morning.

Piano

During its first flight season, the *Hindenburg* carried a lightweight baby grand piano on the deck of its promenade. The piano was made partially of aluminum. It weighed only 397 pounds (180 kg). Captain Ernst Lehmann was sometimes known to play the piano to entertain the passengers.

In the dining room, passengers sat at tables and were served by waiters. The *Hindenburg* had china made especially for the airship. Passengers could purchase a cup with the *Hindenburg* pattern on it as a souvenir.

However, many people complained about the food. American passengers often disliked the German food, to which they were not accustomed. The desserts and cakes were often stale.

After a two-day flight over the Atlantic Ocean, the *Hindenburg* approached the United States on the morning of May 6, 1937. The flight had been normal, and there were no major mechanical problems. The weather had been less than ideal, but it posed little problem for the airship's captains. The strong headwinds put the *Hindenburg* only a little behind schedule. More than anything, the fog simply allowed for less sightseeing than usual.

The passengers awoke that morning eager to make their landing. They packed their things, ate in the ship's dining room, and prepared to land.

A giant map in the Hindenburg allowed passengers to track the airship's progress.

Captain Max Pruss

Explosion in the Sky

The *Hindenburg* came in over Boston, Massachusetts, at approximately noon on May 6. The *Hindenburg* radioed Lakehurst Naval Air Station to inform them of their arrival. The airship had been scheduled to land at 6:00 a.m. that day but was delayed because of strong winds over the Atlantic Ocean.

The weather over New Jersey was also less than ideal. Commander Charles Rosendahl was the senior officer at Lakehurst, a U.S. Navy base. He would monitor the weather conditions and advise the *Hindenburg* on when a safe landing could be made.

AERIAL TOUR OF THE NORTHEAST

Captain Max Pruss decided to bring the *Hindenburg* below cloud level to give the passengers a view of Boston. The passengers were delighted to have a unique view of the area. Those on the ground were just as glad to see the famous airship.

Next, Pruss took the airship over its usual tour of New York City. The crew, ever busy, dropped off the mail it had carried across the ocean. As the airship came in low over the Empire State Building and the Statue of Liberty, the passengers had an excellent view.

The *Hindenburg* also made a low pass over the Ebbets Field baseball

Empire State Building Mooring Mast

The Empire State Building was completed in 1931. As a special design feature, the top of the building could also serve as a mooring mast. Plans to have airships dock to the building never came to fruition. The wind conditions would have made it impossible. Additionally, few passengers would be willing to board or disembark from an airship parked 100 stories in the air.

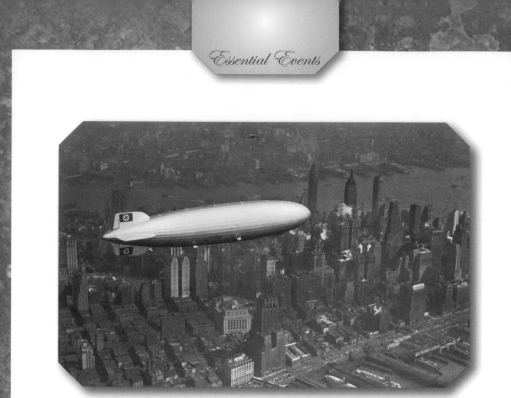

The *Hindenburg* *toured New York City while captain Pruss* *waited for an opportunity to land the airship.*

stadium while a game between the Brooklyn Dodgers and the Pittsburgh Pirates was in progress. As the airship came into view, all eyes turned to the sky. The game stopped while the players and the crowd stood to watch it pass overhead.

DELAYED LANDING

Once Captain Pruss had finished his tour of New York City, it was time for the *Hindenburg* to make its way south to New Jersey. The airship arrived at Lakehurst shortly after 3:00 p.m., but winds were blowing too hard for the *Hindenburg* to attempt a landing. Captain Pruss took the airship out and continued to circle the area, waiting for the wind to calm down.

By 5:00 p.m., Lakehurst had radioed Pruss to tell him the wind had died down, but that visibility was still poor. Commander Rosendahl recommended that the *Hindenburg* further delay its landing until conditions improved. Though eager to land, Pruss agreed to continue the delay. He took the airship northeast toward Asbury Park and then headed south. The airship flew along the New Jersey shore, almost as far south as Atlantic City.

During this delay, chief rigger Ludwig Knoor made an inspection of the gas cells. Knoor thought that the pressure in cell four was low and mentioned it to another crew member. After the landing, they would go over the cell and repair it if they found that it was torn.

Meanwhile, storms had returned at Lakehurst. But the rain stopped shortly after 6:00 p.m., and the sky began to clear. At 6:12 p.m.,

Stormy Weather

Captain Pruss was an accomplished airship pilot. Although the weather was stormy the day the *Hindenburg* was due at Lakehurst, he decided that it was safe to land that evening. Pruss had landed the airship under windy conditions in the past. However, after the explosion, his judgment was called into question. Eckener was reportedly furious at Pruss's decision to land that night.

Rosendahl radioed Pruss, "CONDITIONS NOW CONSIDERED SUITABLE FOR LANDING."[1]

Rosendahl ordered the ground crew to prepare for landing. As the *Hindenburg* made its way back up the New Jersey coast, Rosendahl anxiously radioed the ship again, "CONDITIONS DEFINITELY IMPROVED RECOMMEND EARLIEST POSSIBLE LANDING."[2] He did not want to delay the landing any longer in the event that the storms returned.

Arrival at Lakehurst

The *Hindenburg* returned to Lakehurst shortly after 6:00 p.m. Spectators, photographers, and people who would take the flight returning to Europe watched

The Return Flight

Captain Pruss was not planning to stay very long at Lakehurst after landing. The fully booked return flight was scheduled to leave at midnight. King George VI was going to be crowned as the next king of England on May 12, 1937. Many of those on the return flight planned to attend the coronation. Therefore, it was imperative that the *Hindenburg* deliver these passengers on time.

While the passengers for the return flight waited for the delayed *Hindenburg*, officials from the Zeppelin Company met them at the Biltmore Hotel in New York City. They checked the passengers' tickets and passports and weighed the luggage. They did not, however, subject these passengers to the same thorough search as the flight that left from Germany.

Many of the passengers for the return flight were already at Lakehurst when the *Hindenburg* made its landing. Their eyewitness accounts of the explosion would be important in determining what went wrong that night.

as the *Hindenburg* came into view. The airship's passengers made their way to the promenade and waved to the crowd below. Captain Pruss ordered his crew to prepare for landing.

Rosendahl's men on the ground were prepared and waiting. The ground crew comprised 92 navy men and 139 civilians. Two groups of men, one at the bow and the other at the stern, would grab hold of the landing lines. These steel cables had ropes with wooden handles attached for the men to hold on to. The men would then pull the ship down to its proper height near the ground. Another group was needed to attach the airship to two railroad cars. The airship, attached at the bow and the stern, would then be properly secured.

As the airship approached the landing site, Captain Pruss valved off some of the hydrogen gas. This lowered the ship so that the landing lines would be within reach of the landing crew. Pruss tightly circled the landing field, lowering the *Hindenburg* nearer to the ground.

Civilian Workers at the Air Station

Because so many people were needed to bring in the large airship, it was necessary to hire extra help. Civilians typically made up more than half of the landing crew at Lakehurst Naval Air Station. For their assistance, civilians earned one dollar per hour. Many civilians simply enjoyed being a part of the *Hindenburg*'s greatness. Still, the one dollar per hour they earned could add up on days when the *Hindenburg* was behind schedule.

Many of the passengers on board the *Hindenburg* were eager to land. For many of them, their families were waiting at the airfield at Lakehurst. Most of the passengers were on the promenade looking out the windows during the landing. But the passengers were unable to see what happened when the first explosion took place. Most passengers reported feeling only a small vibration. They knew they were in danger when they saw the ground crew turn to run away from the airship in fear.

Crew members in the front and rear of the airship were ready to drop the landing lines to the ground crew. Hundreds of men on the ground would help steady the *Hindenburg* and direct it to the mooring mast. The wind had not entirely died down at this point, however, and Captain Pruss ordered some of his men to the front of the ship to help balance it.

At 6:25 p.m., the landing lines were dropped. The *Hindenburg* had come to a near stop. Leonhard Adelt remembered:

> Suddenly there occurred a remarkable stillness. The motors were silent and it seemed as if the whole world was holding its breath. One heard no command, no call, no cry.[3]

Almost at that same moment, individuals in the crowd noticed that something strange had happened. A bright flame appeared at the rear of the airship. Within seconds, the flame grew into a massive fire that consumed the airship. The *Hindenburg* was on fire and crashing to the ground.

At approximately 6:30 p.m., the airship exploded and fell out of the sky.

Officials listed the names of survivors on a chalkboard.

Shock and Outrage

*N*ews of the *Hindenburg*'s explosion came
as a surprise to the world. Most people
believed in the superiority of German airships. They
did not think that the *Hindenburg* would be susceptible
to the dangers that had plagued other airships.

The *Graf Zeppelin* and the *Hindenburg* had made more than 600 flights without a single serious accident. The *Hindenburg* had flown in stormy weather and had been struck by lightning. But on May 7, 1937, the world stood in shock as news about the disaster spread across the globe.

HUGO ECKENER AND THE ZEPPELIN COMPANY

News of the disaster reached Germany quickly. A Berlin correspondent from the *New York Times* called Eckener to inform him of the disaster. It was 2:30 a.m. in Austria, only 90 minutes after the explosion at Lakehurst. Eckener was shocked by the news. But in the immediate aftermath, no one seemed to have a clear idea about what had happened.

When the explosion occurred, the *Graf Zeppelin* was in flight on a return trip from Rio de Janeiro. Captain Hans von Schiller received a radio message that the *Hindenburg* had exploded, but he thought it was a joke. Schiller had received a message directly from the *Hindenburg* the night before announcing the ship's safe arrival.

Unfortunately, it was no joke. Schiller received confirmation that the *Hindenburg* had crashed and many people had died. Schiller waited to inform his crew of the disaster until they were over Germany and preparing to land. He broke the news to the passengers only after the *Graf Zeppelin* had made a safe landing.

Eckener ordered the *Graf Zeppelin* to be grounded. Schiller protested that the *Graf Zeppelin* was due back in Brazil in three days. He wanted to continue to operate the airship. But Eckener insisted that the airship remain grounded. He did not want the *Graf Zeppelin* flying until he knew what had made the *Hindenburg* explode.

Eckener left Austria the next morning, on May 8, for Berlin. Eckener was met by reporters in Berlin and suggested that the *Hindenburg* may have been sabotaged. Before leaving for Lakehurst, Eckener met with Hermann Göring, a Nazi general with the Air Ministry. Göring warned Eckener against further mentioning the idea of sabotage in public. The *Hindenburg* was considered a powerful symbol of the Nazi Party. They did not want the public to think that the *Hindenburg* could have been brought down by the party's enemies.

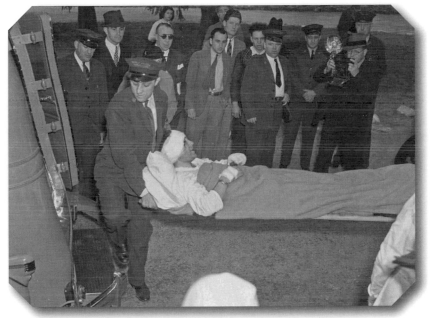

Injured passengers and crew members were taken to nearby hospitals after the disaster.

Shortly after this meeting, Eckener told reporters that his initial idea of sabotage had been premature. He would be meeting with officials in the United States to determine what had gone wrong. He abruptly boarded the ocean liner *Europa* with only the clothes on his back. Eckener was determined to help with the investigation and try to find out what had happened to the *Hindenburg*.

The German people mourned the loss of the *Hindenburg* and the German citizens who had perished on board. In the immediate aftermath, it was not known if anyone had survived the crash. With the *Hindenburg* destroyed and the *Graf Zeppelin* grounded, the future of airships looked grim. But the Zeppelin Company urged the German people to look to the future. The LZ 130 was already in production, and it would be ready to begin making regular flights to the United States in only a few months.

HEADLINES AND NEWS REPORTS

The *Hindenburg* disaster dominated the headlines of every major newspaper in the days following the crash. The front page of the *New York Times* announced to the world, "Hindenburg Burns in Lakehurst Crash; 21 Known Dead, 12 Missing; 64 Escape."[2] Stunning photographs of the explosion and the wreckage were printed on the front pages. Herbert Morrison, a radio announcer, was the only reporter on the scene during the crash. His recording was soon broadcast nationwide on NBC. Audiences were shocked by the newsreel footage of the crash.

Eckener's Guilt

After the crash of the *Hindenburg,* Eckener wrote a letter to his wife expressing his sadness and guilt about the disaster. He wrote, "I deeply regret that I was persuaded to allow the use of hydrogen when the *Hindenburg,* after all, had been designed for the use of helium."[3]

ZEPPELIN BLAST KILLS THIRTY-FIVE

Giant Dirigible Blazing Wreck

Airship Blows Up on Its Arrival at Lakehurst Airport From Germany; Passengers Leap From Burning Ship

LAKEHURST (N. J.) May 6. (AP)—Germany's great silver Hindenburg, the world's largest dirigible, was ripped apart by an explosion tonight that sent her crumpling in the naval landing field a flaming wreck with horrible death to about a third of those abourd her.

Exactly how many died was still in dispute as the flames licked clean the twisted, telescoped skeleton of the airship that put out from Germany several days before on the opening trip of the 1937 passenger season.

The American Zeppelin Company, through its representative, Harry Bruno, placed the death toll at thirty-four of the ninety-seven aboard. The company listed twenty-...

Other news and wirephotos of the Hindenburg disaster will be found on Pages 2, 3, 8, 9, 10 and 4-6 of this section of The Times.

...of the thirty-six passengers and forty-three of the sixty-one man crew as the disaster's survivors.

Allen Hagaman of Lakehurst, who was watching the landing at the mooring mast, also was killed, raising the known toll to thirty-five.

ESTIMATES RANGE TO FORTY

These figures were at slight variance with unofficial estimates of the number of dead which ranged up to forty.

In the crowded hospitals in neighboring communities many of the survivors were in critical condition, a number suffering from excruciating burns.

Some were so gravely injured, among them Capt. Ernst Lehman, that the last rites of the Roman Catholic Church were administered to them.

Lehman, skipper of the ship's 1936 flights, made this ill-fated flight as an observer. Capt. Max Pruss, the commander, was listed among the injured survivors.

CAUSE OF BLAST MYSTERY

What caused the fearful blast, just at the moment the great craft was being moored, no one knew. The explosion occurred at the rear and some observers believed a spark of static electricity following a mooring rope from the ground set off the highly inflammable hydrogen. Other reports indicated a backfiring motor might have sent a...

Storms and buffeting headwinds had delayed the huge ship far behind her schedule for the maiden trip, and slowed down in the early evening to keep the unexpected rendezvous with disaster.

The ground crew of sailors, soldiers and marines moved out into the field to handle her landing ropes.

PASSENGERS IN GAY MOOD

Lower she nosed, her Diesel motors throttled down. Passengers, gayly waving at the crowd, lined the long lounge windows which show like transparent slits in the great silver belly of the ship.

The spider-like web of landing ropes snaked down the little trap doors in the nose. Men of the ground crew grabbed them at the wooden crossbars.

It was 6:25.

Then came the terrific explosion, and brilliant red flames suddenly splashed out toward the stern and the rudder that bore the red-and-black Nazi emblem. The detonation tore the ship as if it were made of paper. The tail dropped earthward.

CRUMPLES DOWN IN FLAMES

The blunt nose bobbed up, hung a moment in the air and then crumpled toward the field, flames running along its sides and the fabric flaking off in big chunks.

Passengers and men of the crew were hurled through the silvered walls of the Hindenburg to the sandy land below. The crowd needed in a panicky surge to the aid of "run for your lives." Navy men dashed into the flame debris to make rescues.

Collapsing in a tangled mass of girders and beams, the ship was torn by a series of smaller explosions, lesser in force than the first shatter...

BLASTS SEND GIANT BALLS OF FLAME SPURTING FROM AIRSHIP

Before the eyes of hundreds of horrified spectators, the giant dirigible Hindenburg exploded in mid-air with a terrific roar over the Lakehurst Naval Air Station yesterday at the completion of a trans-Atlantic journey from Germany. This remarkable picture was taken as one of several explosions sent giant balls of fire into the air from the descending gas bag. The huge Zeppelin was wrecked just as it was about to make fast to the mooring mast which is seen in the photograph.

C.I.O. Joins Film Strike

Labor Council Offer Rejected by F.M.P.C.; Shows to Be Picketed

The Hollywood film studio strike definitely will be on.

This fact was made clear yesterday by Charles Lessing, business agent for the striking Federated Motion Picture Crafts, who said his organization is not at all satisfied with the proposal of the Los Angeles Central Labor Council to end the current institution.

"The strike will continue unless the producers agree to our or union, shop program," he said.

...ped than the powerful the Industrial Organiza-...take a hand, both to...

JURY QUIZZES MRS. SHELBY IN TAYLOR DEATH MYSTERY

Mrs. Charlotte Shelby, mother of Mary Miles Minter, yesterday dramatically denied that she murdered William Desmond Taylor.

She made her first denial in three eighteen interested members here at the Los Angeles county grand jury and told about if later in a crowd of newspaper men in the corridors of the Hall of Justice.

DAUGHTERS QUIZZED

"I was asked if I murdered Taylor and I had to tell them no," she asserted with gesticulations. She paused for breath and continued.

"They asked me if I had any idea who did it and I had to say no again."

Mrs. Shelby was the last of three witnesses to appear before the grand jury during the day...

Survivor Tells Leap to Safety

Blasts Felt Only Slightly, Says One Aircraft Passenger

A survivor's account of the crash of the Zeppelin Hindenburg is given here by one of the passengers of the airship who suffered relatively few injuries.

BY HERBERT O'LAUGHLIN

LAKEHURST (N.J.) May 6. (Exclusive)—I was in my cabin, in the forward section of the Hindenburg, packing my belongings in preparation for the landing that seemed only minutes away, when I felt a slight tremor shaking the ship. That was so slight in...

AGE-PENSION MEASURE VOTED

Assembly Unanimous on Liberalizing Bill

SACRAMENTO, May 6. (AP)—The Assembly today by unanimous vote of 79 to 0 passed and sent to the Senate the Assembly's old-age pension liberalizing measure.

TENTATIVE LIST OF MISSING AND KNOWN CRASH SURVIVORS

LAKEHURST (N. J.) May 6. (Exclusive)—A tentative list of passengers still missing in the Hindenburg disaster and believed dead was compiled tonight as follows:

Rudolf Anders, Dresden, Germany.
R. Herbert Anders, Dresden.

Birger Brinck.
Hermann Doehner, Mexico City.
Donald Curtis, Chicago.
Edward Douglas, New York.
Fritz Erdman.
Otto C. Ernst, Hamburg, Germany.
Mrs. Ernst.
Morita Feibusch, San Francisco.

John Pannes, New York City.
Emma Pannes, New York City.
Otto Reichold, Vienna.
Ludwig Felber and Walter Bernhofer, members of the crew, died of burns in hospitals. They were the only crew members identified among the dead.
Hane Hugo, Leonard Jacobson, Ray Stabler, William Stolt and Franz Wesner, crew members, were listed as missing and believed dead.

LIST OF KNOWN SURVIVORS

News of the Hindenburg *disaster was printed in newspapers around the world.*

Interviews with eyewitnesses and stories of the survivor's harrowing escapes were featured in many newspapers. Captain Lehmann was in the hospital with severe burns. Lehmann did not know the cause of the explosion, but he had been determined to try landing the flaming airship for the safety of those on board and on the ground. The *New York Times* reported that shortly before he died, Lehmann told his doctor:

I intended to stay with the ship as long as I could—until we could land her if possible, but it was impossible. Everything around me was on fire. The windows were open in the central control cabin and I jumped about a hundred feet. My clothes were all ablaze. [4]

Passengers such as Leonhard and

Captain Ernst Lehmann

Ernst Lehmann was a highly respected airship pilot for DELAG. He commanded several airships during World War I. When the Nazi Party became involved in the operations of the Zeppelin Company, it preferred to do its business with Lehmann. Opposed to the Nazis, Eckener was often confrontational. Lehmann was more willing to work with them on their propaganda missions.

Lehmann had been the commanding officer on the *Hindenburg* during its first flight season. But Captain Pruss took over that position for the 1937 season. Lehmann was on board the *Hindenburg* during its final flight, but only as an observer. He wanted to make sure that this flight went smoothly.

Though many of the officers were badly burned during the crash, Lehmann was the only officer to die from his injuries. U.S. Navy officer Charles Rosendahl spoke with Lehmann in the hospital. Lehmann and Rosendahl were good friends and worked together on the airship service flights. When speaking of the disaster, Lehmann told Rosendahl that he thought the ship had been sabotaged. He stated, "It must have been an infernal machine." [6] Lehmann had been working on a book of the history of the *Hindenburg* when he died. Rosendahl completed the work for him.

Gertrude Adelt were employed as reporters. They had been assigned to report on the flight, and their perspectives on the crash would be widely read. Leonhard Adelt described their escape in an article for *Reader's Digest*. Though neither could remember jumping from the airship, they remembered hitting the ground: "We collapsed to our knees, and the impenetrable darkness of black oil clouds shot through with flames enveloped us."[5] Leonhard Adelt's description of the crash and his escape helped many people understand what a desperate situation the people on the *Hindenburg* had faced.

Condolences

President Franklin Roosevelt sent his condolences to Adolf Hitler immediately following the *Hindenburg* crash. Hitler replied, thanking Roosevelt for the aid he supplied to German citizens who survived the crash. This correspondence was a brief friendship between two countries that were highly suspicious of one another during this time.

Funerals began the week following the crash. Memorial services were held in the United States and Germany. When the bodies of the 28 German citizens arrived in Hamburg, Germany, more than 10,000 people paid their respects before the coffins were taken for separate burials.

The *Hindenburg* Movie

A movie called *The Hindenburg* was made in 1975. It starred George C. Scott as the fictional Colonel Franz Ritter and Anne Bancroft as a German countess. In the movie, Colonel Ritter suspects someone on board is planning to sabotage the airship. Though Ritter nearly catches the suspect, the *Hindenburg* explodes at Lakehurst.

The filmmakers used a combination of special effects and newsreel footage to show the explosion. It also helped popularize the theory that the *Hindenburg* was sabotaged. Though the film was a fictional account, it depicts some of the real passengers and crew who were on the flight.

SPECULATION

There was no information about the cause of the crash. None of the crew, passengers, or witnesses had seen anything that clearly would have caused the explosion. Newspapers immediately began to speculate about the cause.

Eckener suspected sabotage. Though he retracted the statement, the theory gained popularity. Newspaper articles speculated about a possible sabotage. People sent letters to the Federal Bureau of Investigation (FBI), claiming to have seen suspicious activity the night of the crash. The writers claimed to have witnessed such things as a small plane flying toward the *Hindenburg* and a man concealing a rifle under an overcoat.

For the most part, these claims were disregarded; the official investigation would soon begin. However, investigators had not ruled out the possibility of sabotage.

A memorial service was held in Germany for the
28 German citizens who died in the disaster.

The cause of the Hindenburg *disaster was under investigation.*

THE INVESTIGATION

The U.S. Department of Commerce began its investigation into the cause of the disaster on May 10, 1937, just a few days after the explosion. With the remains of the *Hindenburg* all but destroyed, it would be difficult to discover the cause of the explosion. But from the beginning, the investigation focused on two main theories. The first was that the *Hindenburg* had been sabotaged. The second theory was that a spark had ignited the hydrogen, causing the explosion.

THE SABOTAGE THEORY

The idea that the *Hindenburg* had been sabotaged was popular among the public and with good reason. The *Hindenburg* was a symbol of Nazi power, and the Nazi Party had made many enemies in the United States and in Germany. This made the *Hindenburg* a likely target for those who opposed Hitler's Nazi regime.

The inspection prior to takeoff was intended to reveal a bomb. However, Kathie Rauch, the woman who wrote a letter warning of a possible explosion, had no real information regarding the incident. Rauch had merely seen the explosion in a psychic vision.

The sabotage theory was ultimately played down by both German and U.S. investigators. This was due, in part, to the Nazi Party's unwillingness to be portrayed as vulnerable to attack. Several members of the *Hindenburg* crew, however, believed sabotage

Investigators had few clues that pointed to a clear cause of the disaster.

to be the only possible explanation. While many people belonging to the Zeppelin Company publicly rejected the idea of sabotage, they privately confided their belief that it was the only explanation. Their experience working on the airship and their faith in its construction made them disregard suggestions that the crash was the result of faulty engineering.

Airships had survived lightning strikes and bullet holes in the past; they had flown through all kinds of weather. It seemed unlikely that any of these things could be the cause of an explosion this time.

However, the U.S. investigation ultimately ruled out the possibility of sabotage. After looking at the passengers and crew and interviewing witnesses, investigators found no evidence of a bomb. Investigators also failed to find anything to suggest a plot among Nazi dissenters to bring down the airship. Without any evidence of sabotage, investigators moved on to the next likely explanation: mechanical failure.

Spark Theories

One theory was that an electric spark started the fire on the *Hindenburg.* Some investigators assumed that a spark might have ignited hydrogen that had been valved off to lower the airship and caused the explosion. Others considered the possibility that there was a hydrogen gas leak on the airship. As the *Hindenburg* was coming in to land, it made a sudden sharp turn. These investigators speculated that the turn caused a cable in the airship to fracture and cut into one of the gasbags. They believed that a spark then ignited the gas escaping from the gasbag.

Although the storms had broken by the time the *Hindenburg* was preparing to land, many believed that the static electricity in the air could have caused the spark that ignited the fire. Airships typically build up a static electric charge during their flights. With storms in the area, the charge may have been greater than normal. When the ship was grounded, the buildup of static electricity could have been discharged as a spark.

Another theory for the source of the spark included a backfired engine when the engines were put in reverse to stabilize the airship. The spark might also have occurred because of friction. St. Elmo's fire was also considered a possible source of the fire, given the weather conditions that night. St. Elmo's fire is a phenomenon that occurs most often

St. Elmo's Fire

St. Elmo's fire is believed to be a possible source of the electric spark that ignited the fire on the *Hindenburg*. However, no witnesses in the investigation reported seeing St. Elmo's fire at the time of the disaster.

during thunderstorms. An electric discharge causes the surrounding atmosphere to glow.

Results of the
U.S. Investigation

At the public inquiry into the cause of the *Hindenburg* disaster, witnesses from the airship's crew and passengers, as well as witnesses on the ground, testified to what they saw that night. Many reporters also attended the inquiry. Eckener and other officials from the Zeppelin Company were also present. They were aiding the U.S. investigation, but they were also conducting their own private investigation.

The interviews revealed that the fire began near gas cell number four. But the cause of the spark that started it was more difficult to determine. Rosendahl testified that the landing lines had been lowered, grounding the ship, for a full four minutes before the fire began. He also said that the sharp turn that the *Hindenburg* made before landing was not unusual. Such maneuvers help keep the airship level when gas and water ballasts are being released for landing.

Testimony from other crew members cast doubts on the idea that the spark came from the engines. The engines were not reversed until well after the hydrogen had been valved off. This allowed the gas to dissipate. Also, hydrogen gas is released from the top of the airship, far away from the engines below. Crew members also reported that the landing lines were dry, which would have made them poor conductors of electricity.

Eckener testified for the inquiry as well. Though he was not present at the disaster, Eckener was familiar with the workings of the airship. He had listened to the testimony of eyewitnesses and crew, and he had investigated the crash site. Eckener told the committee that he believed the crash had occurred because of the sharp turn the *Hindenburg* made just before landing. A wire bracing the rudder could have broken during the turn and ripped open a gas cell.

Although none of the crew reported seeing any mechanical failures, investigators believed that an electric spark must have ignited

The German Investigation

Germany carried out its own investigation into the cause of the *Hindenburg* crash. The German team's findings were similar to those of the U.S. investigation. However, the official report listed eight probable causes for the fire—including sabotage.

the hydrogen. In the end, the U.S. investigation concluded that a hydrogen leak near cells four and five had been ignited by an electric spark. They said that the source of the spark was probably St. Elmo's fire. This, they said, was the most likely explanation.

THE ZEPPELIN COMPANY

The sight of the *Hindenburg*'s wreckage devastated Eckener. He told Rosendahl:

> *Stretched out across the centre of the field lay the blackened framework of the Hindenburg, a disorderly tangle of girders, wires, and crumpled sheet metal. It appeared to me the hopeless end of a great dream, a kind of end of the world, a mournful symbol of what I expected to be the final outcome for Germany.*[1]

After the crash, the future of the Zeppelin Company was in question. Another disaster like this could not occur. Zeppelins would need to be filled with helium if they were to continue to fly. But Adolf Hitler's Nazi regime was growing more powerful. By 1938, it was clear that Hitler intended to go to war. President Roosevelt's Commerce Secretary Harold Ickes refused to approve the sale of helium to a German company. Ickes disliked the Nazis and their policies. Roosevelt never asked Ickes to reconsider his decision.

The LZ 130 was completed in 1938 and named the *Graf Zeppelin*. The original *Graf Zeppelin* had been retired. But the new airship was often called the *Graf Zeppelin II*. With no helium available, the Nazis agreed to use hydrogen to inflate the airship. The Nazis used the *Graf Zeppelin* for training and propaganda flights and occasionally for spy missions.

However, as war was approaching, the Nazis had no real use for the zeppelins. Airplane technology had greatly advanced since the end of World War I, and the zeppelins were too vulnerable to attacks. The zeppelins were dismantled and used for airplane parts.

Bain's Theory

In 1997, a new theory on the *Hindenburg* disaster emerged. Addison Bain, a hydrogen expert for NASA, had reexamined the cause of the *Hindenburg* crash. Looking at newsreel footage, Bain said that the fire did not appear to be a hydrogen fire.

After the *Hindenburg* caught fire, it hung in the air for several seconds before it began to crash. Bain says when it finally fell, the bow bounced when it hit the ground. According to Bain, if the hydrogen had been the first thing to catch fire, it would have been the first thing to burn up and the *Hindenburg* would have crashed swiftly.

Bain believed that it was not the hydrogen, but the outer cover of the *Hindenburg* that first caught fire. After Bain received a piece of the *Hindenburg*'s original cover, he tested it. The paint, or doping agent, used to strengthen the fabric was highly flammable. The Zeppelin Company had selected the paint for its silvery, reflective appearance.

Eckener and the U.S. Navy

Although Germany had given up on the airship, the U.S. Navy still hoped to continue developing an improved airship. The airships would be for both military and commercial use. In 1946, just after the end of World War II, J. Gordon Vaeth, a U.S. Navy reserve lieutenant, traveled to Germany to speak with Eckener.

Vaeth found the 77-year-old Eckener in his home near Lake Constance. When he arrived, Eckener remarked, "I didn't know who it would be, but I was sure that sometime someone in the U.S. Navy would get in touch with me."[2] The two spoke about rebuilding the airship industry. In April 1947, Eckener traveled to the United States to consult with the Goodyear Aircraft Corporation. They made plans to build a 950-foot- (289.5-m-) long luxury aircraft that could carry 252 passengers and 180,000 pounds (81,647 kg) of cargo. But when they could not find financial backers for the project, it was abandoned.

Eckener returned to his retirement in Germany. He kept in touch with his friends around the world, and he remained interested in political affairs in Germany. Eckener died on August 14, 1954, at the age of 88.

However, it contained chemicals similar to those in jet fuel. Bain says that a static electric shock could have ignited the *Hindenburg*'s cover. Once the fire grew, it spread to the interior of the ship and ignited the hydrogen, which further fueled the raging fire.

Although Bain's theory was the first new theory on the disaster that had gained popularity in some time, it was eventually discounted. Many people still affirm that hydrogen played the central role in the *Hindenburg* crash.

THE FUTURE OF AIRSHIPS

Although the idea of building rigid airships was abandoned, nonrigid blimps continue to be used in the United States. During World War II, the U.S. Navy used blimps for convoy escort and coastal patrol. It employed blimps as part of its cold war defense system. In the 1970s, during the energy crisis, blimps

The End of the Zeppelin

Many people see the *Hindenburg* disaster as the moment that marked the end of the airship. However, airship Captain Pruss saw it differently. He said, "It was not the catastrophe of Lakehurst which destroyed the Zeppelin; it was the war."[3]

became popular again. They were used to transport cargo.

Blimps are an efficient way to transport items long distances because they can do so without having to refuel. They are also useful in reaching remote areas of the world. Many places do not have airports or are not easily accessible by other means. Blimps are often able to reach these areas to transport supplies or passengers.

After nearly 60 years, the Zeppelin Company announced its plans to build a new airship. After the *Graf Zeppelin* was dismantled and the large air hangars were destroyed, the Zeppelin Company continued to operate as a manufacturing company. The Zeppelin-Metalwerk Company made metal objects, such as radio antennas and aluminum containers. But in its return to airships, the Zeppelin Company planned to build a new rigid airship. The Zeppelin NT (New Technology) is smaller than the older zeppelins at 246 feet (75 m) and uses helium as the lifting gas. NT airships can hold two pilots and twelve passengers. This new type of airship is used for leisure flights.

On September 18, 1997, the Zeppelin NT 07 made its first flight. The company has built four airships. The NT 07 is no longer in operation, but the company has airships operating in Germany, Japan, and the United States. The U.S. zeppelin operates out of San Francisco, California, and made its first flight on May 21, 2008.

Though they are not the rigid airships Eckener dreamed of, the Zeppelin Company is on its way to producing a fleet of passenger airships. Eckener's dream may yet become a reality. ⌒

Today's Blimps

In the United States, blimps are often seen flying above major sporting events. These blimps are smaller, at 182 feet (59 m) long, and are used to provide unique camera angles.

Zeppelin NT 07

TIMELINE

1783	1852	1863
The first hot-air balloon is flown in France.	Henri Giffard achieves the first powered, dirigible flight on September 24.	Count Zeppelin takes his first hot-air balloon ride in St. Paul, Minnesota, on August 19.

1914	1917	1919
World War I begins in Europe.	Count Zeppelin dies on March 8.	Germany signs the Treaty of Versailles on June 28 and gives up its airships.

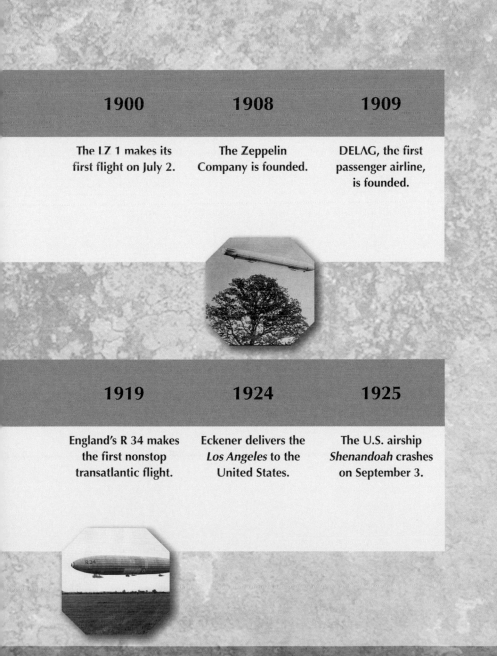

1900	1908	1909
The LZ 1 makes its first flight on July 2.	The Zeppelin Company is founded.	DELAG, the first passenger airline, is founded.

1919	1924	1925
England's R 34 makes the first nonstop transatlantic flight.	Eckener delivers the *Los Angeles* to the United States.	The U.S. airship *Shenandoah* crashes on September 3.

TIMELINE

1929

The *Graf Zeppelin* completes its flight around the world.

1930

The British airship the R 101 crashes on October 5.

1937

The *Hindenburg* leaves Germany on May 3 for its first flight of its second flight season.

1937

The *Hindenburg* catches fire and crashes at Lakehurst Naval Station on May 6.

1933

Adolf Hitler becomes
chancellor of
Germany.

1936

The *Hindenburg*
makes its first trial
flight on March 4.

1937

On May 10, the
U.S. Commerce
Department begins an
investigation into the
cause of the crash.

1937

The U.S. investigation
determines that a
hydrogen leak and
static electricity
caused the fire.

Essential Facts

Date of Event

May 6, 1937

Place of Event

Lakehurst Naval Air Station, Lakehurst, New Jersey

Key Players

- ❖ Count Ferdinand von Zeppelin
- ❖ Hugo Eckener
- ❖ Adolf Hitler
- ❖ Captain Ernst Lehmann
- ❖ Captain Max Pruss
- ❖ Herbert Morrison
- ❖ Commander Charles Rosendahl

Highlights of Event

❖ The United States refused to sell helium to other countries, which forced the Zeppelin Company to use hydrogen as the lifting gas in its airships.

❖ Before the *Hindenburg* took off, a letter claimed that there was an explosive device on the airship. Security personnel searched the airship and all of its passengers before takeoff. They did not find any explosives on the airship.

❖ Stormy weather delayed the *Hindenburg*'s landing.

❖ The weather cleared shortly after 6:00 p.m., and U.S. Navy Commander Charles Rosendahl radioed the *Hindenburg* to return for landing.

❖ The *Hindenburg* caught fire just before landing and it was quickly engulfed in flames.

❖ The U.S. investigation determined that a static shock ignited the hydrogen in the *Hindenburg* and caused the explosion.

Quote

"She was to be an airship in which one would not merely fly, but would also be able to voyage."—*Hugo Eckener*

ADDITIONAL RESOURCES

SELECT BIBLIOGRAPHY

Archibold, Rick. *Hindenburg: An Illustrated History*. New York: Warner Books, 1994.

Botting, Douglas. *Dr. Eckener's Dream Machine*. New York: Henry Holt and Company, 2001.

Dick, Harold G., and Douglas H. Robinson. *The Golden Age of the Great Passenger Airships: Graf Zeppelin & Hindenburg*. Washington DC: Smithsonian Institution, 1985.

Hoeling, A. A. *Who Destroyed the Hindenburg?* New York: Popular Library, 1962.

FURTHER READING

Lace, William. *The Hindenburg Disaster of 1937*. New York: Chelsea House Publishers, 2008.

Majoor, Mireille. *Inside the Hindenburg*. New York: Little Brown and Company, 2000.

McCaffrey, Jill. *The Hindenburg*. New York: Chelsea House Publishers, 2001.

Web Links

To learn more about the *Hindenburg* disaster, visit ABDO Publishing Company online at **www.abdopublishing.com**. Web sites about the *Hindenburg* disaster are featured on our Book Links page. These links are routinely monitored and updated to provide the most current information available.

Places to Visit

Navy Lakehurst Historical Society
PO Box 328, Lakehurst, NJ 08733-0328
732-244-8861
www.nlhs.com
Visit the site of the *Hindenburg* crash and learn about airships. A memorial in honor of those who died in the disaster is located on the base. A memorial service is held each year on May 6.

Smithsonian National Air and Space Museum
Independence Avenue at Sixth Street, Southwest
Washington, DC 20560
202-633-1000
www.nasm.si.edu
The museum features exhibits on the history of flight, including the role of airships.

Smithsonian National Postal Museum
2 Massachusetts Avenue North East, Washington, DC 20002
202-633-5555
www.postalmuseum.si.edu
The museum features an exhibit on the role of the *Hindenburg* in the U.S. Postal Service. Damaged mail from the final flight is on display.

GLOSSARY

airship
A large aircraft, airborne by lifting gas, such as hydrogen or helium, and powered by motors.

bow
The front of a ship.

dirigible
An airship able to be controlled or steered.

dissenter
A person who disagrees with the opinions of the majority.

dope
A varnish applied to fabric to make it stronger or airtight.

girder
A large metal beam used to build large structures.

helium
The second-lightest chemical element; not flammable.

hydrogen
The lightest chemical element; highly flammable.

icebreaker
A ship designed to break a passage through ice.

incendiary
Designed to cause fire.

propaganda
Biased information used to promote a political cause.

psychic
The ability to read minds or see the future.

St. Elmo's fire
> Phenomenon when an electric charge appears on objects near the sky.

static electricity
> An electric charge produced by friction.

stern
> The rear of a ship.

swastika
> A symbol of the Nazi Party.

transoceanic
> Able to travel across an ocean.

zeppelin
> An airship made by the Zeppelin Company.

Source Notes

Chapter 1. Oh! The Humanity!

1. Herb Morrison. "The Crash of the *Hindenburg.*" NBC Radio broadcast. May 6, 1937. Reprinted in Garner, Joe. *We Interrupt This Broadcast: Relive the Events That Stopped Our Lives.* Naperville, IL: Sourcebooks, 1998. "'The Crash of the Hindenburg'." *American Decades Primary Sources.* Vol. 4: 1930–1939. Detroit, MI: Gale, 2004. 507–511. *Gale Virtual Reference Library.* Gale. Minneapolis Public Library. 7 Oct. 2008 <http://0go.galegroup.com.mplwebcat. mplib.org:80/ps/start.do?p=GVRL&u=mnpminn>.

2. Ibid.

3. George Willens. *We Saw the "Hindenburg" Disaster!* Detroit, MI: George Willens, 1937 Burton Historical Collection, Detroit Public Library, Detroit, MI. "'The Crash of the Hindenburg'." *American Decades Primary Sources.* Vol. 4: 1930–1939. Detroit: Gale, 2004. 507–511. *Gale Virtual Reference Library.* Gale. Minneapolis Public Library. 7 Oct. 2008 <http://0go.galegroup.com.mplwebcat.mplib.org:80/ps/start. do?p=GVRL&u=mnpminn>.

Chapter 2. Lighter Than Air

1. Rick Archbold. *Hindenburg: An Illustrated History.* New York: Warner Books, 1994. 10.

Chapter 3. War Machine

1. Douglas Botting. *Dr. Eckener's Dream Machine.* New York: Henry Holt and Company, 2001. 66.

2. Ibid. 62.

3. Rick Archbold. *Hindenburg: An Illustrated History.* New York: Warner Books, 1994. 49.

Chapter 4. The Future of Air Travel

1. Rick Archbold. *Hindenburg: An Illustrated History*. New York: Warner Books, 1994. 102.
2. Ibid. 110.
3. Douglas Botting. *Dr. Eckener's Dream Machine*. New York. Henry Holt and Company, 2001. 196–197.

Chapter 5. The Greatest Airship

1. Douglas Botting. *Dr. Eckener's Dream Machine*. New York: Henry Holt and Company, 2001. 266.

Chapter 6. Up Ship!

1. Douglas Botting. *Dr. Eckener's Dream Machine*. New York: Henry Holt and Company, 2001. 272.

Chapter 7. Explosion in the Sky

1. Rick Archbold. *Hindenburg: An Illustrated History*. New York: Warner Books, 1994. 178.
2. Ibid.
3. Ibid. 181.

SOURCE NOTES CONTINUED

Chapter 8. Shock and Outrage
1. Rick Archbold. *Hindenburg: An Illustrated History*. New York: Warner Books, 1994. 196.
2. Ibid. 193.
3. Douglas Botting. *Dr. Eckener's Dream Machine*. New York: Henry Holt and Company, 2001. 285.
4. "BURNS ARE FATAL TO CAPT. LEHMANN," *New York Times (1857–Current file)*. Retrieved November 5, 2008, from ProQuest Historical Newspapers The New York Times (1851–2005) database. (Document ID:94372294).
5. Rick Archbold. *Hindenburg: An Illustrated History*. New York: Warner Books, 1994. 188.
6. Douglas Botting. *Dr. Eckener's Dream Machine*. New York: Henry Holt and Company, 2001. 287.

Chapter 9. The Investigation
1. Douglas Botting. *Dr. Eckener's Dream Machine*. New York: Henry Holt and Company, 2001. 288.
2. Ibid. 297.
3. Ibid. 294.

INDEX

INDEX CONTINUED

ABOUT THE AUTHOR

Jill Sherman is the author of three books in the Essential Library series. She has also contributed to many other books for young people. She holds a BA in English from the College of New Jersey.

PHOTO CREDITS

Popperfoto/Getty Images, cover; AP Images, 6, 45, 46, 51, 55, 56, 63, 64, 66, 72, 75, 98 (top), 99; Murray Becker/AP Images, 10, 15, 71, 82, 86, 95, 98 (bottom); Library of Congress, 16, 21, 25, 26, 35, 96 (top), 97 (top); Hulton Archive/Getty Images, 29, 96 (bottom); Jimmy Sime/Getty Images, 36, 97 (bottom); Central Press/Getty Images, 39; Time Life Pictures/Mansell/Getty Images, 61; American Stock/Getty Images, 77; Anthony Camerano/AP Images, 81